BECAUSE I'M THE CHILD HERE AND I SAID SO

A Joke Book for Parents
(Because You Need a Laugh!)

PAT BYRNES

**Andrews McMeel
Publishing**

Kansas City

To Rebecca.
May you never recognize your mommy and daddy
in this book.

Five of the cartoons in this book originally appeared
in *The New Yorker*.

06 07 08 09 10 11 WKT 10 9 8 7 6 5 4 3 2 1

ISBN-13: 978-0-7407-5738-9
ISBN-10: 0-7407-5738-5

Library of Congress Control Number: 2005932616

www.andrewsmcmeel.com

INTRODUCTION

This book is no mere collection of silly cartoons. No, good parent, it is a serious manual for modern child rearing, however cleverly disguised. Though it was initially devised as a practical resource for my own (fairly recent) foray into parenthood, it should serve equally well any other parent, new or advanced, seeking the clearest, most concise instruction available amid an ever-proliferating array of options.

This is not to slight the volumes devoted to parental instruction. They are indeed vital to modern child care. You see, we live in an age of not only scientific, but also highly competitive, parenting. The right book can make all the difference. It could hold that elusive secret that might possibly, maybe, if we're lucky, give us the edge over that brat's parents down the block. To risk being without it could bring embarrassing failure from which our children might never recover. More importantly, neither would we. Because our children are, after all, a reflection of ourselves.

God help them!

The books, no matter how they disagree on the particulars, all say essentially the same thing: "You're doing it wrong." That is, if you don't do it their way. As if the slightest deviation will cause your child to explode. Or, worse, lose ten IQ points. Their primary purpose, from what I can gather, is to make us hopelessly paranoid parents, crippled by feelings of inferiority and utterly dependent upon buying more and more books.

So I present this book as an antidote to the others. Oh, it says basically the same thing—"You *are* doing it wrong"—but only if you are doing it this way. None of these cartoons show the way we are parenting. Rather, they depict the way we see *other* parents doing it, but are too polite to correct. So sit back and *enjoy* a parenting book for once, free of that nagging sense of inferiority. Savor the comforting, long-overdue balm of acknowledged superiority. And restore all that sapped self-confidence in raising happy, healthy children. I guarantee it will be worth at least ten IQ points.

BECAUSE I'M THE CHILD HERE AND I SAID SO

"Just remember, son, it doesn't matter whether you win or lose—
unless you want Daddy's love."

"Can't you up his dosage or something?
I mean, he's still daydreaming."

"A birthday party? Didn't we already do that kind of crap with your older sister?"

"I'm sorry, Tommy, you've been voted out."

P. BYRNES.

"Think of all the obese children in America."

"They make clear duct tape now,
so it's hardly even noticeable."

"I couldn't find a sitter, so I got a video."

"Your mother and I just don't feel we were cut out to be parents.
But you're still free to stay with us."

"How's Mommy's little disappointment?"

"Because I'm the child here and I said so."

"Have that Ritalin ready."

"I said I wanted to learn the banjo. What did you do?"

"Average?! You mean he has a learning disability?"

"I'm sorry, sweetie, but not this weekend.
Mommy and Daddy have to attend a parenting conference."

"Can I go outside and play? . . . Just kidding. What's on TV?"

"He'd threatened me with 'the belt' before, but I must have really ticked him off to get the pants as well."

"Can you hold? I want to tuck in my kids on the other line."

"Put down what and play with who?"

"I burned out on stimulation at thirteen months."

P. BYRNES.

"She already knows two words: 'Mama' and 'Who?'"

P. BYRNES.

"You're an only child because we loved you
and wanted you to remain our favorite."

"I'm out of Ritalin. Got a quarter?"

"I'll be the mommy and you be the baby.
Now here's a video; I have some things to do."

"So what were we supposed to do, leave it in the car?"

"Will you turn that TV down?
Can't you see I'm on the phone?"

"We'll be fine, as long as your parents die before they get to college."

"We have a nanny for when we can't take the baby
and a sherpa for when we can."

"Interactive: That's the word for when nobody
wants to deal with you, so they get a machine to do it."

P. BYRNES.

"I don't get it, either, why some women insist on
home preschooling their children."

"What do I have scheduled after my nap?"

"It shuts them up."

"We're totally committed to giving her the best child care minimum wage can buy."

"Eat up—you need those. They have lots of B vitamins for stress."

"But I'm telling you, *es mi casa. Estoy su papa.*"

"Think of discipline as another form of stimulation."

"At least I convinced them to watch the Discovery Channel."

"We're not really going to start talking colleges
until the third trimester."

"Okay, it's nap time. All cell phones off;
switch pagers to vibrate."

"What do you want to watch, my 'Best Of' or outtakes?"

P. BYRNES.

"Remember, you're here to see and be seen and not heard."

"Until I'm old enough for surgery,
can I at least wear falsies?"

"She has my old nose."

"I think it's straight As, but could you read it to me?"

"He made the game-winning play,
and I failed to get it on video."

"We packed up the van and drove across the country where we saw, like, fifty DVDs."

"He's really quite gifted, just not in any verifiable way."

"But this is tap water. I wanted toilet water."

"The government won't let us carry them in front anymore."

"I talked to my kids about discipline. You?"

"Before Ritalin, I couldn't even get through
a simple video game."

"We looked at a number of styles and colors
before settling on the orange jumpsuits."

"But it's the Grand Canyon! You can't hit 'pause' for the Grand Canyon?"

"This, Jared, is called a 'sedan.'"

"Mr. and Mrs. Peters! You're home early."

"I'm sorry, but we're trying to raise Stephanie
in a Disney-free environment."

"I got kicked off the team for good sportsmanship."

"Hey, doofus, your underwear's not showing."

"It's like being online with God."

"I saved all your father's old e-mails."

"Quit trying to fast-forward Grandma."

"I won the spell-check bee."

"I know. We need to work on his abs."

"The food here is served dysfunctional family-style."

"We adopted her in China, and we're
having her raised there, too."

It begins

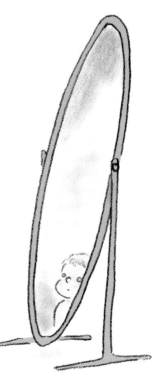

P. BYRNES.

"Everyone in my class is Shamiqua, Taylor, or Ashley.
How'd I get stuck with a weirdo name like Mary?"

"Teenagers! Everyone try to look cool!"

"That's how. I asked, Why?"

"I don't have math problems. I have math issues."

"We adopted a quack baby."

"That's the 'undo' button."

"Think of it as an intelligence-gathering mission."

"He's 95th percentile for drooling."

"When I was a kid, we had to push a button."

"It's just baby talk, but it's baby talk in *French*."

"Are these your original parents?"

"Would you like to hold the baby?"

"You mean I was grown hydroponically?"

"But Prince Charming was the sperm donor, right?"

"I'm suing my parents for not instilling in me
a sense of common decency."

"Don't give up your day school."

"Ew, no. Brittany's a name for old ladies with tattoos."

"I've got to know—is this a real play date or are we just friends?"

"Lord, bless us and keep us safe on our journey,
especially as we get within twenty-five miles from home,
where most accidents occur."

"No fair. Jimmy Lartner listens to Raffi instead of Mozart, and he gets the same grades."

"Don't talk to me about sex. My generation invented sex."

"She's average, and that's what makes her special."

The author wishes to acknowledge his lovely wife, Lisa, for making parenthood possible, and his charming agent, Linda Langton, for making this book possible.